ARNHEM

ARNHEM

A CASE STUDY

Maurice Tugwell

foreword by
GENERAL SIR JOHN HACKETT
GCB, CBE, DSO, MC, B.Litt, MA, LLD

BOOK CLUB EDITION

Photographs by courtesy of the Imperial War Museum
Maps by Christopher Fayers

Printed by The Anchor Press Ltd, Tiptree, Essex
Bound by Wm Brendon & Son Ltd, Tiptree, Essex

© Maurice Tugwell 1975

This edition published by Purnell Book Services Limited,
St. Giles House, 49/50 Poland Street, London W1A 2LG,
by arrangement with Thornton Cox Limited.

Contents

List of Illustrations and Maps

Foreword

by General Sir John Hackett, GCB, CBE, DSO, MC, B.Litt, MA, LLD

It is unlikely that airborne forces – ground forces, that is, delivered into the area of the battle by means of aircraft – will ever again be used as they were in World War II. The piloted aircraft as an instrument of war soared into the military firmament like a rocket from its take-off in the early nineteen-hundreds, through its rise towards high significance in World War I, to its apogee in World War II. The light emitted on its journey is splendid still. Future historians, however, may well find somewhere in the mid-twentieth century the point at which its decline began, at about the same time that the introduction of weapons of mass destruction made it clear that all-out war between major powers was no longer a rational act of policy. The piloted aircraft continues to play a dominant part in major wars waged directly between minor powers, and in minor wars waged indirectly between major powers. In these the use of airborne forces is still important. We are almost certainly beyond the point, however, at which the state of the art in movement by air and defence against it will permit of the deployment of airborne divisions in operations conducted directly by one major power against another. Huge, slow moving aerial armadas composed of troop-carrying prime-movers and towed glider transports, such as that which darkened the sky in south-east England on 17 September 1944, are unlikely ever to be seen again. The half century in which, in the context of a major war, the complete airborne operation became a possibility, was nearly realized (though never quite), and then appeared a possibility no longer, is over.

The airborne operations of World War II, partly because they are of a sort unlikely now to be repeated and partly in spite of it, can be expected to attract the interest of students of war for some time yet to come, and none more perhaps than the operation known as 'Market Garden'. The separability of this operation as a coherent whole from, so to speak, the rest of the war, the shortening of a world war which might have resulted from its success, the dramatic conjunction of mischance and mistake which marked its course, and the notable conduct of many who fought in it all combine to make of 'Market Garden' a particularly interesting problem in war and a specially inviting subject for study. It has shown itself to be particularly attractive to the historical journalist, as distinct from the serious historian. The piece of analysis now before us is the work of a writer with claims to be in the second category and deserves, short though it is, to be taken seriously.

There are many problems in this operation which are still only partially solved. I propose to identify here some of the areas in which they lie.

The first concerns planning. Of all the three Divisions, that most dangerously exposed, the British First Airborne, had good claims to priority in airlift resources. Since the greater part of these belonged to another ally, however, the satisfaction of these claims would not have been easy. Moreover, the development of early momentum in the advance of XXX Corps as it followed up the airborne assault demanded early success in the operations to secure the crossings over water obstacles further south. There is no doubt, however, that the spreading out of the delivery of First Airborne over several days, with loss of surprise after the first, was a major factor in the whole operation's failure. Another was the distance of dropping and landing zones from objectives. The senior officers in the parachute brigade coming in on the second day were aware that to advance, against opposition already aroused, to objectives 8 miles from the DZ as the plan demanded, was quite impracticable. They knew that the battle would not work out this way. It is argued that the air force commanders should have been prepared to accept a higher degree of risk from the anti-aircraft defences in the vicinity (notably those protecting Deelen airfield), which turned out in the event to be less formidable than was feared.

There is certainly still something more to be said about this. Another debatable point is whether, given the disinclination to accept increased flight hazard, more use should have been made for dropping purposes of the polder country south of the Lower Rhine.

Why, it must also be asked, was so little attention paid to intelligence material from several sources indicating the presence of at least the cadres of two Panzer Divisions in the area? Why was the advice of the Dutch not sought, and when proffered disregarded, on the best line of approach for XXX Corps to Arnhem? It is not only in hindsight that the single bund road, running northwards from Nijmegen, so easily interrupted by anti-tank weapons, does not appear to be the best tank route to Arnhem. Dutch officers who had made staff studies before the war were mystified when the Guards Armoured Division was pushed on up this road. Their own conclusions had favoured the system of secondary roads running north-west to the Rhine, and thereafter upstream, on both banks if possible.

These are among the questions which arise in connection with the planning of the operation. Others arise in connection with its execution.

It is now clear that the biggest single adverse factor affecting the course of the battle fought by the British First Airborne Division for the chief prize in the whole operation, the bridge at Arnhem, was an almost total failure in command at divisional level for a day and a half at the most critical period of the battle. Urquhart, almost from the time of his arrival on 17 September, was virtually out of wireless communication with the Brigade whose task was to secure the bridge. Why this was so is still not quite clear, but the equipment appears to have been unable to work satisfactorily in unfavourable local circumstances. Uninformed criticism has suggested that it should have been tested beforehand in a similar environment but there was not time for this and the Division had in any case already been alerted at short notice for a good many other operations in quite different environments. The equipment was, however, inadequate and Urquhart did the only thing possible. He went forward. By dismal bad luck, he was then pinned down, incommunicado, in company with the

Brigadier who was his chosen replacement in the event of his becoming a casualty. By the time Urquhart got back to his HQ and resumed control, 39 hours later, it was too late for critical decisions which he alone could take, while indecision and procrastination had dispersed the last chance of a co-ordinated drive to get through to Frost, at the bridge, a force made up out of the greater part of four battalions available and at hand only a mile or two away.

Urquhart, if in effective command, could have made several critical decisions. He could have decided to bring down the whole of 4 Parachute Brigade on arrival to push towards Frost. He could have decided to hold the critical high ground at Westerbouwing and the heavy ferry at Heveadrop, even at the cost of abandoning the Arnhem Bridge, and concentrate all the remaining resources of the Division, still formidable, on holding this bridgehead west of Oosterbeek. He could have chosen a better location for a battle headquarters and a better area for a defensive battle than those he found himself landed with when he came back. If he had decided to push a force through the town to Frost late on the 18th he would have been able to give it the coherence, the impetus, and the single command which was needed, instead of allowing this last chance of supporting Frost to vanish in muddle and delay. When he got back to his HQ on the morning of 19 September this was in fact almost the first thing he tried to do, but it was too late.

Other things went wrong in the execution of the plan. Divisional communication rearwards was as bad as forward to brigades. Air supply arrangements, hampered by bad weather, were not well handled at command levels and even matchless courage by aircrew could do little to put things right. It would not be difficult to find other instances of maladroitness and mischance. The final question remains. Should the operation have been called off when evidence began to mount that success was unlikely? The author of this essay thinks not. I believe, partly for reasons he gives and partly for others, that he is right.

Preface

AIRBORNE WARFARE IS the child of the Second World War. Invented by the Italians, developed by the Russians, parachute troops were first used in action by the Germans in 1940 and '41. Those were the years when the *Wehrmacht*, brilliantly led, scored a series of dazzling victories over neighbours that neither wanted war nor prepared themselves adequately for defence. In Norway, Belgium, Holland and Crete these victories were hastened or accomplished by one division of paratroops, one brigade of glider assault troops, and an infantry division trained to be landed in the battle area by troop-carrier aircraft. Enjoying the advantages of surprise and shock effect, supported by fighters and dive-bombers which during daylight hours offset their lack of heavy support weapons, often operating against poorly equipped opponents, these *Fallschirmjäger* proved the value of the airborne method.

But in Crete it was also demonstrated than when surprise assaults failed to seize objectives the task of capturing them by deliberate attack was often beyond the very limited offensive capability of the airborne men. Victory was there clawed out of near defeat because the mistakes of certain Allied commanders provided the German airborne leader, General Kurt Student, with an opportunity to land his airborne reserves at the point of Allied weakness.

The lessons of 1940 and '41 were clear enough. Airborne tactics depended for success upon the exploitation of surprise; upon really intimate co-operation between the air force – both troop-carriers and fighter-bombers – and the airborne soldiers; upon the ability of the commander to influence the outcome by committing reserves to meet the needs of battle; and upon the fighting qualities of the troops. And one further, sombre fact was evident. Against an experienced, determined enemy, especially in terrain where he could use his tanks, the whole concept of airborne warfare was hazardous in the extreme.

This last consideration caused the Allies, in 1943 and the first half of 1944, to limit their airborne attacks to the close support of surface operations. In both the Sicily and Normandy landings the British and American airborne troops seized objectives inland of or adjacent to the assault beaches. It was as though a duellist, seeing that his opponent was wearing armour, used his delicate rapier to jab at the chinks instead of trying to run him through. This was sensible in the circumstances; nevertheless some senior Allied commanders, including Field-Marshal Montgomery, appreciated that at the right moment, when the enemy was off balance and temporarily disorganized, Anglo-American airborne forces might be used with as much daring as the *Fallschirmjäger* in their heyday.

This is the story of the sole Allied attempt in the war against Hitler's Germany to exploit such a fleeting chance and plunge the airborne rapier through their weakened adversary.

I

The Bridge

SOME OF THE fires had burnt themselves out, leaving charred timber and gutted buildings, but many houses still blazed fiercely, victims of recent fighting. Eighteen, maybe twenty acres of town lay in ruins but the bridge remained intact, a visible symbol of hope to its hard-pressed defenders. A massive structure of concrete and steel, it spanned the River Rhine and carried the road on a raised extension into the southern part of Arnhem.

The condition of the men holding this valuable military objective was hardly less grim than the state of the wrecked houses from which they conducted their defence. Three days earlier they had flown from their camps in England and parachuted onto Dutch soil nearly 70 miles behind the German front line. After assembling they had set off as planned along the seven miles of road separating their drop zone from their objective and, after a series of fierce skirmishes, had seized the northern end of the bridge just after daylight faded. Unable to capture the southern end of the bridge because of German guns firing point-blank, these men of the 2nd Parachute Battalion and attached units of 1st Airborne Division formed a tight defence on both sides of the northern road extension. From this bridgehead they could deny use of the bridge to the enemy, whilst holding it open for the tanks of the Guards Armoured Division, due to relieve the isolated paratroopers. Now, 72 hours after capturing their objective, in the late afternoon of 20 September 1944, they were hanging on more by a mixture of determination, discipline, pride and loyalty than by any tactical advantage or actual military strength. All around them lay dead German soldiers, scattered between knocked-out tanks and armoured troop-carriers, testimony of bitter fighting against fearful odds.

In battle, men are frequently subjected to nervous strain – excitement, fear, anticipation; and often they are short of sleep and proper food, so that fatigue weighs down upon them making it difficult to remain alert, to think clearly or to exercise the care necessary for survival. One or other of these influences dominates at any moment – imminent danger stifles fatigue, then weariness overcomes fear – a grinding routine in any form of combat, multiplied tenfold for the small band of airborne soldiers who had fought almost non-stop for three days against the growing strength of German tanks, guns and infantry. When the Germans sealed off the road by which Lieutenant-Colonel John Frost's men had reached the bridge, the group numbered nearly 700. Now the force was reduced to under two hundred still in action. Many of this number were wounded, but capable of continuing: so long as a man was capable, he fought. They were nearly but not quite exhausted, almost but not completely without ammunition, capable of withstanding a few more attacks, but only just. Men with blackened, grime-covered faces peered out of the ruins, bloodshot eyes on the lookout for a sniping tank, or for infiltrating infantry; and now and then the eyes turned south across the river, hopefully scanning the landscape for any sign of the Guards tanks.

These had been due the previous day, according to the timetable so confidently announced at the briefings. They did not appear, but a radio message was received to the effect that the relief force would reach the bridge by 5 pm on the 20th, the fourth day of fighting. As the paratroopers looked at their watches and saw the deadline tick by, and later as dusk settled upon that desolate scene, they came quietly to terms with a grim reality: for reasons unknown to them, the plan had miscarried. They had not been relieved 'within 48–72 hours'; all the indications were that the tanks would never arrive in time. This was the second disappointment the defenders had been obliged to swallow. The first arose during the second day, when it became clear that reinforcement units from the main body of 1st Airborne Division were apparently incapable of breaking through to the bridge from their positions west of Arnhem. It had been said of British soldiers in an earlier heroic military adventure –

'Theirs not to reason why
Theirs but to do and die.'

Few of the men at the bridge attempted to reason why: they cursed their luck and carried on. Their part in the battle had been achieved – the bridgehead had held firm for longer than the stipulated period. Now all they could do was hold it a little longer, to do and, if necessary, to die, leaving it to others to explain how it was that no tanks had arrived from the south; and why, out of 1st Airborne Division's 10,095 men and 96 guns safely landed to the west of Arnhem, only 700 men and four 6-pounder anti-tank guns had ever reached the divisional objective – the bridge at Arnhem.

II

The Concept

ON 10 SEPTEMBER 1944 three commanders of airborne divisions had stood around a large map of Holland while their corps commander, Lieutenant-General F. A. M. Browning, gave orders. Major-General Maxwell Taylor and Brigadier-General James Gavin, commanding respectively the 101st and 82nd United States Airborne Divisions, were briefed in that order, which took the listeners from south to north up the map, progressively deeper into enemy-held territory. Finally General Browning drew a circle round a town near the extreme north of the map and turned to address Major-General Roy Urquhart, commanding the British 1st Airborne Division.

'Arnhem Bridge,' he said tersely, 'and hold it.'

The 1st Airborne Division* consisted of Brigadier Gerald Lathbury's 1st Parachute Brigade, whose fighting qualities had led the Germans in Tunisia to name its soldiers *Roten Teufeln* – Red Devils; Brigadier 'Pip' Hicks's 1st Airlanding Brigade, glider-borne troops who in 1943 had landed near Syracuse in Sicily; Brigadier 'Shan' Hackett's 4th Parachute Brigade, which had fought as infantry in Italy but had never jumped into action and, under command for the forthcoming operation, Major-General Stanislaw Socabowski's newly formed Polish Parachute Brigade. In addition there were gunners, sappers, signals, medical and service units and a light reconnaissance squadron mounted on jeeps. General Urquhart had taken command eight months earlier. Although hardened in the stern school of infantry command in the Middle East he had no previous airborne experience, opinion at

---

* 1st Airborne Division's Order of Battle is reproduced at Appendix 1.

the time inclining to the view that any good fighting soldier could easily pick up the threads of this form of warfare. But if an airborne division can be likened to a rapier, then an infantry division resembles a mace; the techniques of their use differ.

The battle plan described by General Browning required I Airborne Corps to seize crossings over the rivers and canals that separated the British Second Army from its objective, the Zuider Zee, thus laying what has been termed an 'airborne carpet' for the ground troops. This was Operation Market. The water obstacles included the Maas, the Waal and the Rhine. It was across the last river that the bridge at Arnhem carried the road north towards the final objective, and this was nearly 70 miles from Second Army's front line. As soon as these air-landings started, Lieutenant-General Brian Horrocks's XXX Corps was to strike north along the 'carpet' – Operation Garden – until a corridor had been cleared into a lodgement area north of the Rhine. There the armies might wheel right and sweep into the heart of Germany, to victory in 1944. The combined operation was called Market Garden, and it was to start on 17 September.

When Field-Marshal Montgomery had pressed the proposal on his Supreme Commander, General Eisenhower, the Germans had only one weak division, with virtually no reserves, holding their front in Holland. This was the rare and fleeting opportunity in which the type of operation envisaged stood a good chance of success. The enemy had suffered a shattering defeat in France, losing most of his army in the west, and was vulnerable to a knock-out blow. Already the Allied armies had pursued the retreating *Wehrmacht* in the south across the Moselle and in the north over the Somme. But although in August and early September 1944 the British and American divisions seemed irresistible, their continued offensive ability was in fact severely restricted by a shortage of supplies. All their needs – fuel, ammunition, food, vehicles and equipment – were being brought to the Continent through Cherbourg or across the invasion beaches, and sufficiency was unlikely to be achieved until additional ports, particularly Antwerp, were brought into use.

There were two broad courses of action open to the Supreme Commander: to consolidate, open more ports, build up a sound logistic backing, and then develop operations employing the full weight of the Allied Forces on a broad front; or to concentrate all immediately available supplies and support behind one offensive and try to knock the groggy opponent out before he had time to recover. There was merit in both. Unfortunately, the decision to back Montgomery's plan was delayed, and the backing when it came was within the framework of a broad front strategy and consequently fell short of the total commitment needed: Market Garden fell between the two valid courses of action. The delay was the most serious matter. By the second week of September the Germans had improvised and moved forward *Generaloberst* Student's First Parachute Army, and this stood between Horrocks and the Rhine. Also, by chance, II SS Panzer Corps was refitting north and east of Arnhem. Although well below strength in tanks and men, the 9th and 10th SS Panzer Divisions that formed *SS Obergruppenführer und General der Waffen SS* Wilhelm Bittrich's Corps were battle-experienced and shrewdly led, and represented a serious threat to any lightly armed and equipped airborne men who might land within their reach. The conditions still made Market Garden a reasonably sound investment, but only if both the airborne and the ground offensives went like clockwork. What then had gone so very wrong, between the first briefing on 10 September and the desperate plight of the small airborne force holding Arnhem Bridge ten days later? What answers can now be given to the questions: why were the tanks of XXX Corps not there to relieve the bridgehead; and why had the defence of the bridge to be conducted by less than one fourteenth of the airborne force that had been landed with that specific mission?

III

The Ground Advance

AT 1330 HOURS on 17 September, shortly after the airborne landings had begun, the tanks of the Irish Guards led the XXX Corps attack up the road towards Arnhem. A moving barrage of artillery shells fell ahead of them as three hundred and fifty guns lent support. From well-sited positions German anti-tank batteries engaged the armour with their 88 mm guns, inflicting losses. Two hundred RAF Typhoon fighter-bombers roared in to silence those anti-tank weapons that had been spotted by the guardsmen and the attack pressed forward. Operation Garden was from the outset a desperately hard-fought advance. Across the flat, low-lying Dutch landscape, the tanks and their support vehicles were restricted to the roads. These were raised above the flooded fields, presenting all that moved upon them with the utmost clarity in the German gunners' sights. Originally envisaged as a lightning thrust, brushing aside the flimsy defences existing at the beginning of September, the operation in practice called for an apparently endless series of awkward, bitter battles. Awkward because, by the nature of the terrain, proper deployment of tanks off the road, where their superior mobility and fire-power would have proved irresistible, was impossible; bitter because every man from General Horrocks to the youngest guardsman knew that each hour of delay diminished hope of relieving the paratroops.

Fortunately, the Americans of the 82nd and 101st Airborne Divisions had seized all but one of their vital objectives. Thus the airborne carpet carried the Guards Armoured Division – Horrocks's leading element – over all the water obstacles between their start-line and Arnhem, bar one. The massive bridge spanning the River Waal at Nijmegen remained firmly in German hands. General Gavin had been given a series of tasks beyond the capa-

21

city of his or any other division. Appreciating this, General Browning had made it clear at his briefing that the Waal bridge was to be given lowest priority, and was to be seized only if this could be done without risking other missions. German reaction was very sharp indeed, and Gavin had insufficient spare capability to capture the Waal bridge. The Guards reached Nijmegen on 19 September. Had they been given a free run across the Waal, hope would still have existed that they might reach Arnhem by noon the next day, within the 72 hours maximum forecast. But it was dusk on the 20th when a superbly gallant and successful combined US Airborne and British Armoured attack secured Nijmegen bridge. An important factor in this achievement was the German inability to reinforce their Waal defences, because their panzers were north of the Rhine, and the British Airborne held the Rhine bridge.

The Guards Armoured Division has been criticized for attacking by daylight only and failing to maintain the momentum of their advance throughout the drive to Nijmegen, thus wasting valuable hours and providing the German defenders with time to prepare defences for the next day's fighting. Again on the night of the 20th, a hush fell over the battlefield. Nine miles further north time was running out for the defenders of Arnhem Bridge. By dawn on the 21st, when the armoured attack re-started, that defence had crumbled. In fact the advance on the 21st failed to penetrate the German force occupying the Betuwe – the island between the streams of the Rhine and the Maas. On the 22nd Horrocks pushed his 43rd (Wessex) Division into the lead, hoping that infantry might succeed where tanks had failed. This they did, but not without difficulty, and it was night when the leading battalion reached the south bank of the Rhine. The point they made for was not the Arnhem road bridge; it was five miles away, south-west from a small town called Oosterbeek. They headed in that direction because it was known that the bridge was no longer in British hands; and because immediately north of the Rhine, in a narrow perimeter running a mile and a half north from the river bank, what remained of the 'main body' of 1st Airborne Division was fighting desperately for its life. We must now turn back the pages to discover how it was that this Division was fighting this battle five miles removed from its objective.

IV

The Airborne Plan

WHEN ON 10 SEPTEMBER General Urquhart walked slowly back to his caravan from General Browning's briefing, the exciting prospect of leading his Division into the most challenging airborne assignment in history was to some extent clouded by two problems to which Browning had alerted him. One was the shortage of troop-carrier aircraft to lift his Division; the other, the belief that German air defences in the Arnhem area prohibited landings close to the bridge on either side of the river. His mission however was straightforward, and well within the capability of the force under his command. With his Chief of Staff, Charles Mackenzie, and in co-operation with his RAF opposite number – Air Vice-Marshal 'Holly' Hollinghurst who commanded the RAF troop-carriers – he set to work on his divisional plan.

Airborne planning is best done back-to-front. One starts with the ground tactical plan, which is the end-product of the whole operation. Having decided where you want your units to fetch up, you next make the landing plan, which should serve the ground action by delivering troops and equipment at the place and time most likely to enable ground objectives to be seized. Since surprise is vital, it usually follows that dropping and landing zones should be as close as possible to the objectives. Finally there are the air movement and marshalling plans. Within the former, the important decision for the army commander is how to use available air-lift, that is the allotment of priorities between units, and between manpower on the one hand and heavy weapons, vehicles and equipment on the other. Air force considerations are bound to affect the landing and air movement phases. Sometimes a conflict of opinion will arise between the army and air force commanders over, for instance, time and place of landing. Ideally this should be resolved by the officer in overall command, in this case Browning, balancing one set of risks against another and arriving at a decision binding upon both services.

Urquhart's ground tactical plan required 1st Parachute Brigade to hold the bridge; 4th Parachute Brigade to occupy the high ground immediately north of Arnhem; and 1st Airlanding Brigade and the Polish Parachute Brigade to take up positions on the western and eastern outskirts of the town respectively. Field and anti-tank artillery was to strengthen the defence. Who can doubt that this plan, had it been put into effect, would have succeeded in holding Arnhem bridge intact for XXX Corps, even if their advance had taken twice as long? The reasons why it was numerically only one-fourteenth effective were that the landing and air movement plans failed to support it, and because the planned use of reserves was inflexible.

Possible landing and dropping zones existed in an open area cut up by ditches immediately south of the bridge; in a clearing north of the river two miles to the east; on heath-land south of the airfield at Deelen, four miles north of Arnhem; and in a large stretch of firm, dry ground north of the river, on average some seven miles to the west. Deelen airfield was known to be defended by *Flak** artillery, and bombers passing over Arnhem had reported being fired on from the area of the town. The information on flak was, however, very sketchy. Dutch liaison officers warned that the zone south of the bridge was too soft for glider landings, besides being intersected by drainage ditches.

Urquhart was agreeable to abandoning the northern zone because it clearly involved unreasonable risk. He also accepted that the southern and eastern areas were unsuitable for landing gliders *en masse* and decided to send these to the spacious but more distant zones further westward. He remained anxious to get 1st Parachute Brigade onto the Arnhem bridge with the minimum loss of surprise, and he asked the RAF to drop the Brigade both sides of the river as close as possible to the bridge. This was unacceptable to the Air Force: flak on the run in, or on the exit

---

* '*Flak*', German for anti-aircraft, was adopted for slang usage by the Allies.

routes, or both, was regarded as too great a hazard for the vulnerable troop-carriers and their paratroop passengers. This was a valid consideration and it called for a decision, which ought ideally to have been made by Browning, between on the one hand accepting the risks from flak in order to land close to the objective, and on the other, minimizing landing hazards by using only the western zones, at the risk that the bridge might be demolished before capture and that without benefit of surprise the task of seizing the objective might be costly and difficult.

Criticism has been levelled at General Urquhart for accepting the RAF viewpoint without first raising the issue formally with his Corps Commander. General Browning, however, knew all about the conflict of opinion and the potentially serious consequences for Operation Market. Either he shared Urquhart's view that the risks involved in landing so far from the objective were acceptable or he knew that he, no more than his subordinate, could shift the RAF from their position. Although in overall command of the ground operation, Browning did not exercise authority over the troop-carrier force. After the Sicily landings a joint War Office–Air Ministry memorandum had decreed that 'airborne operations are air operations and should be entirely controlled by the Air Commander-in-Chief'. Thus the senior RAF officer, free from responsibility for the outcome of the ground battle, could nevertheless decide how the force should be landed. With the benefit of hindsight, which enables us to know the many difficulties that were to confront 1st Airborne Division (not least II SS Panzer Corps about which Urquhart had very little knowledge), we may be tempted to suggest that the divisional commander ought to have told General Browning that, unless part at least of his force could be landed close to the objective, the operation should be abandoned. But at the time so drastic a course was really out of the question.

Throughout the Normandy fighting 1st Airborne Division had been held in reserve, being alerted for no fewer than 16 operations, all of them cancelled. If one can imagine being called forward 16 times for an ordinary commercial flight, only to be told of successive postponements, it is possible to guess the effect on the division of the cancellations. Urquhart recorded that 'there were already signs of that dangerous mixture of boredom and cynicism creeping into our daily lives'. Operation Market was being planned in England on the basis of what proved to be over-optimistic information about the enemy, and the impatient para-troops, infected by the general mood of the nation that the war was as good as won, were ready and willing to accept any task and almost any risk to see something of the action before it was over. Our hindsight enables us to see how serious a mistake it was to land the entire division seven miles or more from its objective: but if on Urquhart's advice the Arnhem operation had been called off, would not we, with our modified hindsight, see him as lacking initiative, determination and 'airborne spirit'? How his officers and men might have seen him does not bear contemplation. If there is blame to be apportioned, Browning and Hollinghurst must share it with Urquhart: but where the fault really rested was on an unsatisfactory system of joint responsibility that denied overall command to any one officer.

The air movement plan was governed by two principal factors: the shortage of troop-carriers, and the inability of the American aircrews to operate with assured accuracy by night. The British airborne troops had at their disposal 149 USAAF and 130 RAF C-47 Dakotas, and 240 converted RAF bombers. Of the latter, 38 were taken by Browning to tow gliders of his advanced Corps headquarters, a decision more easily understood in human than in strictly military terms. This deprived Urquhart of one batta-lion's lift. Even so, considering that the bombers would tow the 29 passenger Horsa gliders, or the even larger Hamilcars, the airlift available to 1st Division was greater than that allotted to either American division in terms of men or material that could be delivered in the first wave. But whereas the 82nd and 101st US Divisions each devoted more than three-quarters of their lift on the first day to infantry, the 1st Division decided to allot only half its capacity for this purpose. Thus each American division could hope to end the day with three brigades in action, while the British plan* introduced only 1st Parachute Brigade and the 1st Air-landing Brigade, the latter less two companies, to battle on 17

* 1st Airborne Division's allotment of aircraft and gliders to units, by lifts, is set out in Appendix 2.

September. It would seem that the British staff, planning an airlift composed predominantly of gliders, allowed their units the luxury of all the jeeps, motor cycles and heavy gear that the gliders could carry, disregarding the imperative needs of battle – a small number of carefully selected heavy loads and lots and lots of fighting soldiers.

Although Air Vice-Marshal Hollinghurst and General Urquhart disagreed over place of delivery, they were united in their efforts to achieve two lifts in the first day, thereby reducing to a minimum the disadvantages of too small a troop-carrier force. But in this endeavour they were opposed by General Brereton, whose First Allied Airborne Army was made up of all the Allied airborne troops and troop-carriers. Aware of his American crews' limited abilities in night operations, Brereton vetoed the two-lift proposal because it would have involved some night flying, and because of crew fatigue. So the landing and air movement plans had to cater for a second lift on 18 September and, as there would still be a Brigade uncommitted, a third lift on the 19th.

Subject to elimination of flak in its vicinity the RAF had accepted the zone south of the river for parachuting, giving it the code letter 'K'. So, from 18 September onwards, the delivery of reserves to the battlefield could be via either the western zones or DZ 'K'. Unfortunately the planning of these lifts was unimaginative and wooden, throwing away the advantage that air mobility bestows on airborne reserves – the ability to influence the outcome of a battle by their timely and appropriate introduction. A timetable was appointed, requiring 4th Parachute Brigade and the balance of air-landed troops to land on the morning of the 18th on the western zones; and the Poles to land on DZ 'K' on the 19th. How much better to have issued tentative orders only, with the warning that all reserves must be prepared at short notice to respond to whatever instructions might be radioed from the battle area. One of the consequences of this plan was that Urquhart saw the need to retain half the infantry delivered in the first wave – the Airlanding Brigade – to protect the western zones. This left him only 1st Parachute Brigade, a quarter of his total force, to achieve the divisional mission during the first 24 hours.

Arrangements for close air support of the airborne troops during the forthcoming battle were woefully inadequate. No proper liaison was established with 83 Group, RAF, whose fighter-bombers operated over Holland; air control teams were few, poorly trained, and equipped with radios which in the event never worked; and General Browning acquiesced to an Air Force ruling which barred 83 Group from supporting his Corps whenever troop-carriers and their escorts were due overhead the battle area.

So of the four lessons from the successful German airborne operations of 1940 and '41, three were neglected in the planning of Arnhem. Surprise was surrendered; air force co-operation, troop-carrier and fighter-bomber, was insufficiently close; and the commander's ability to influence the outcome by the skilful use of reserves went by default. Only in the fighting quality of its troops and aircrews was 1st Airborne Division on a par with the *Fallschirmjäger*. But the opposition awaiting them was in an altogether different class from anything which had confronted the German paratroops.

V

German Defences

AFTER THE WAR it was suggested that Operation Market had been betrayed to the Germans by the Dutch traitor, Cristiaan Antonius Lindemans. Such intelligence as he provided was in fact thought by the Germans to be unreliable and was in any case received too late. It was luck, that fickle saboteur or kindly assistant, that provided the Germans with a complete set of I Airborne Corps' plans.

The main stream of Allied troop-carriers passed directly over *Generaloberst* Student's headquarters. The man who had led the *Fallschirmjäger* in their glorious days gazed with envy at the majestic armada passing overhead. While he was telling his chief of staff how he wished that so powerful an airborne force had been at his disposal, a platoon of his men were searching the wreck of one of 82nd US Division's gliders shot down just to the north. The plans were found on a dead officer's body; within a few hours these were spread out on Student's desk. So from the first evening the German command knew the strength, dispositions and intentions of the Allied airborne divisions.

Student's superior commander was *Generalfeldmarschall* Walter Model, the outstandingly capable and experienced officer recently appointed to command Army Group B, the more northern of the two German army groups in the west. Model's headquarters was at Oosterbeek, between Arnhem and the western landing zones. He had been about to sit down to lunch when a message was received that Allied airborne landings were taking place two or three miles to the west. He immediately ordered the HQ to be moved and departed for Arnhem where he paused at *Generalmajor* Kussin's Area headquarters to report the situation to Berlin before continuing to Doetinchen – headquarters of Bittrich's II SS Panzer Corps.

Model and Bittrich were quick to appreciate the threat posed by 1st Airborne Division's landings. They agreed to order *Oberst* Harzer's understrength 9th SS Panzer Division to reconnoitre in the direction of Arnhem and Nijmegen, to occupy the Arnhem area and to attack and destroy the British forces. 'The aim', the instruction summarized, 'is to occupy and firmly hold the bridge at Arnhem.' 10th SS Panzer Division was ordered to contain the Americans south of the Waal in Nijmegen. Later, when the captured plans were known to them, these officers remained satisfied that, with only minor modification, their orders could stand.

Meanwhile Kussin set off in his staff car to see for himself the position and actions of the British. On the road west he came upon *SS Sturmbannführer* Sepp Krafft, CO of an SS Training Battalion. Krafft explained how he had reacted to the reported landings by deploying his small force as a frail screen between the landing zones and Arnhem, in an attempt to delay movement and collect detailed intelligence. After approving these measures Kussin took the road to Oosterbeek. It was to be his last journey.

VI

The Landings

THE LANDINGS OF the British first wave had gone almost faultlessly. The fog over English airfields had cleared in time for 0945 hours take-offs, and weather conditions were generally good. Of the 320 gliders that set off 39 failed to reach their destinations, due to flying hazards and technical failures. No aircraft or glider in the British first lift was lost through enemy action. 1st Airborne Division's leading element was Major B. A. Wilson's Independent Parachute Company – the pathfinders. Their role required them to jump 20 minutes prior to 'H' hour and mark the landing and dropping zones to make their recognition easier for the aircrews of the main force. Wilson recalled: 'I shall always remember that lovely Sunday morning. Everything looked so peaceful. There were cows feeding quietly in the fields and peasants going about their work. Not a sign of fighting or war. Not a glimpse of the enemy.' But hardly had he remarked to his pilot on the quietness of the journey than their Stirling aircraft was rocked by anti-aircraft shells bursting nearby. Soon he was leading his men through the six-feet-long floor aperture into the slipstream. The men's parachutes, connected to a strong-point inside the plane by webbing straps, were pulled open automatically as they fell the length of the straps. Soon the soldiers were swinging earthwards through light small-arms fire. Two men were hit in the air. Wilson landed and discarded his parachute in time to accept the surrender of a German soldier. This man led him to a platoon position where a number of other dispirited soldiers were glad to give themselves up. The pathfinders set up their beacons, marked the zones and waited anxiously for the main force. Presently the throb of engines announced the arrival of 1st Airlanding Brigade and divisional glider elements. The wind on the LZs was lighter than expected, causing a number of gliders to overshoot and end up in trees. Two Hamilcars that touched down on soft soil nosed over. But that was the limit of misfortune; on the whole the glider landings on 17 September were more successful than on any previous large-scale operation or exercise. So too was the descent of 1st Parachute Brigade. The American C-47 (or Dakota) transports flew in tight formation nine abreast. Nineteen para-troops jumped from each and the drop was accurate and concen-trated. Surprise had been complete, landing casualties few, and almost everyone began the battle in the right place at the right time. Thus far, the decision to use only the zones several miles west of Arnhem seemed to be justified.

As soon as his men had assembled Lieutenant-Colonel John Frost set off with his 2nd Parachute Battalion for the Arnhem road bridge. The plan had envisaged the Divisional Reconnaissance Squadron making a preliminary dash for the objective. Several of the Squadron's jeeps were loaded in gliders that failed to reach the battle area, but those that were available set off through the woods and villages towards Arnhem. None got through. This sacrifice of the divisional reconnaissance element would mean that no proper probing could be conducted of the enemy screen between the landing area and the bridge, with time-consuming and costly consequences for the infantry who were trying to get to the objective.

Frost's Battalion advanced along the road running close to the north bank of the River Rhine, 3rd Parachute Battalion by a more direct route a little to the north, and the 1st Battalion by a more northerly course still to occupy the high ground just north of Arnhem. Dutch civilians poured out of their houses to welcome them, causing some delay, and the peaceful atmosphere of the drop zones continued for the first mile or two of the march. Then the advancing paratroops clashed with the screen of SS troops hastily deployed by *Sturmbannführer* Krafft and the whole operation became influenced by the friction of war. Initially the opposition was light, but all the time Krafft's men were being reinforced by tanks, half-tracks, guns and infantry of Harzer's 9th SS Panzer Division. This German division's tasks included the security of the

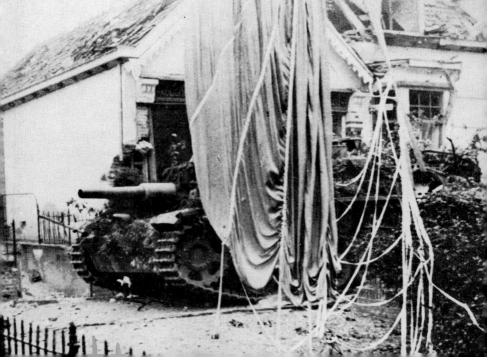

Arnhem road bridge. So, as the daylight faded on 17 September, two divisions were moving under orders to seize the bridge at Arnhem – the British 1st Airborne and the German 9th SS Panzer. But whereas the Germans were aware of their opponents' general position and probable intention, the British were still completely ignorant of the SS formation's existence, let alone its plan.

On the central and northern approaches the 3rd and 1st Parachute Battalions were slowed down by enemy resistance. Almost the first Germans encountered by the 3rd drove in a staff car headlong towards their leading company. The paratroops staged an improvised ambush and the occupants were all killed within seconds. Amongst the dead was *Generalmajor* Kussin.

VII

Conflict

AFTER LEAVING HIS glider Major-General Urquhart watched the drop of 1st Parachute Brigade onto the adjacent DZ and then made his way to the spot at the edge of a wood where his tactical divisional headquarters was setting up. It was here that he became aware of a new and very serious problem: radio communications were simply not working. In the sandy, well-wooded terrain, the radio sets provided for airborne operations were proving completely inadequate. Neither within battalions, nor between battalions and brigade headquarters, nor within the divisional network was radio communication good, and on many it was non-existent. The same applied to the several links to HQ I Airborne Corps near Nijmegen and the air support organization. The result was to be paralysis within the Division, just as severed nerves paralyse the human body. Realizing that he could exercise no control over the battle from a headquarters out of radio contact, Urquhart set off in his jeep to visit subordinate units. After seeing that the glider battalions had the security of the landing zones well in hand he made his way along 2nd Parachute Battalion's southern route towards Arnhem. He found that Frost was up with his leading platoon personally supervising the destruction of a German outpost that had delayed the advance. So he left a message of encouragement with the battalion headquarters and, after withdrawing from the immediate battle area, switched routes to find the 3rd Battalion. Urquhart caught up with the 3rd at the crossroads where Kussin lay dead. Here he found Brigadier Lathbury who had also decided that, without efficient radios, he must get forward to the action. The 3rd Battalion was soon held up and became somewhat disorganized and exhausted as a result of its efforts to break through. Built-up areas enormously favour defence. An advance through streets against determined opposition is invariably a slow and costly experience, especially if support by heavy weapons and by the air force is lacking. This was 1st Airborne Division's problem. German mortars ranged onto the crossroads and inflicted casualties. As night drew on, Urquhart agreed with Lathbury to halt the 3rd Battalion for the time being with a view to continuing the advance at first light on the 18th. In his account of the battle General Urquhart recorded his misgivings at this moment: 'Now I realized that I was losing control by being away from my own HQ. I was dissuaded from returning as this would have meant passing through areas which were not in our hands. After some searching moments I decided that at least I was now with the brigade charged with the initial thrust to the Bridge and thereby usefully placed to give on-the-spot instructions.' While the 1st and 3rd Parachute Battalions were finding their progress towards Arnhem blocked, and were suffering severe casualties in their endeavour to proceed, the 2nd Battalion on the southern route was faring better. Here a flaw was discovered in the rapidly improvised German positions. Lieutenant-Colonel Frost, veteran of airborne actions in Bruneval, North Africa and Sicily, led his splendidly trained and determined men towards his objective, crushing opposition *en route*. The rail bridge, some three miles west of the main road bridge, was a secondary battalion objective. C Company turned right to seize this, Lieutenant Barry and his platoon being the first to reach the river bank. They had set foot on the bridge when the enemy fired demolition charges which destroyed it. In the words of one of the soldiers present 'it seemed to curl back on us'. Barry and two men were wounded by the blast. C Company then made for another objective – a building in Arnhem believed to contain a German headquarters. In the subsequent fighting they were separated from the remainder of the Battalion and were never able to break through to rejoin them.

The main body of 2nd Battalion meanwhile continued towards the road bridge. From a dominating feature called Den Brink, machine guns opened fire upon them. Frost had anticipated this, and B Company were briefed to clear this area while A Company resumed the advance. This plan succeeded, although it resulted in B Company becoming temporarily detached. So it was that Major Tatham-Warter's A Company led the headquarters and support elements of the 2nd Battalion towards the steel outline of the bridge, fading as dusk fell across the confused scene. Surprisingly, in view of the high importance attached to the bridge by Generals Model and Bittrich in their orders, the Germans had neglected to reinforce its close defences. There were traffic police at the northern end and, at the southern, flak artillery and pillboxes. Tatham-Warter's men moved rapidly and silently along the now darkened streets to reach the northern bridge extension. He immediately despatched a platoon to capture the southern end. This and later attempts were thwarted by intense fire from the pillbox and flak guns, now firing point-blank along the open roadway. At the same time the houses on either side of the northern end were occupied and prepared for defence. 'We would knock on the door of a house,' an eyewitness recalled, 'and be instantly met by the earnest prayers of its inhabitants not to billet ourselves on them. Seeing our preparations for defence, they would then say most politely "surely you are not going to fortify this house?" To which I would reply, equally politely "I'm afraid I am".' In this unreal atmosphere of a peaceful town plunged suddenly into war, the 2nd Parachute Battalion and the divisional troops which had accompanied them prepared to fight one of the epic battles of the Second World War.

VIII

Crises

THROUGHOUT THE NIGHT 17/18 September the Battle of Arnhem hung in the balance. The British landings had achieved surprise and the operation had got off to a good start. The Germans, benefiting from the chance disposition of II SS Panzer Corps, from the prompt and intelligent reaction of base units in the battle area, and from the accurate assessment of British intentions made by Bittrich and soon confirmed by Student's captured orders, had partially frustrated the 1st Division's intentions. Only partially, because the 2nd Battalion held the north end of the road bridge. Given early re-inforcement this British advantage might become decisive; but early re-inforcement by troops already in Holland was unlikely because of the difficulty being experienced by 1st and 3rd Parachute Battalions in penetrating the German defensive screen. The failure of communications was depriving these efforts of cohesion and support, and the failure to provide really close and continuous air support weakened the Division's offensive capacity. Thus handicapped, 1st Division on the battlefield was in some difficulty.

Its strength lay in its uncommitted reserves – the 4th and the Polish Parachute Brigades and the balance of divisional troops. Fresh and eager for battle, these formations provided the means of restoring a situation fraught with danger and of regaining the initiative. In spite of radio failures one fact was becoming abundantly clear to the staff officers at 1st Division headquarters – the Germans had successfully halted the advance of the main body from the western zones towards Arnhem. Next morning, the 18th, 4th Parachute Brigade plus divisional troops were due to be dropped on the same DZs. No one seems to have questioned the wisdom, in circumstances quite different from those envisaged in

37

planning, of reinforcing failure. DZ 'K', south of the bridge, was marked on the aircrews' maps ready for use on the 19th. No technical difficulty need have prevented its use on the second day and the radio link from 1st Division to the UK Base was among the few that worked. All that was required was a command decision, communicated in forthright terms, to switch 4th Brigade to the point of crisis – DZ 'K' and the bridge. Such an adjustment would also immediately have freed 1st Airlanding Brigade from their unproductive role of guarding the landing areas. But neither Urquhart nor Lathbury, who understood the difficulties encountered by 1st Brigade, was in a position to issue orders; the Corps Commander, General Browning, was near Nijmegen and out of radio touch with 1st Division; and the staff at divisional headquarters, lacking in their orders any hint of flexibility in the use of reserves, were hamstrung. So the hours of darkness ticked away, and with them, the unique opportunity to re-shape the plan of battle. Left undisturbed, this plan was to lead to 4th Parachute Brigade's virtual annihilation four miles west of its objective, a fate to be shared by almost the whole Division.

Dawn on 18 September saw a sharp and successful engagement involving the 2nd Parachute Battalion, now well established at the northern end of the bridge and reinforced by a half company from the 3rd Battalion, some divisional engineers, the headquarters of 1st Parachute Brigade less the Commander, Major Freddie Gough of the Reconnaissance Squadron, and other small detachments. Obeying Bittrich's orders, Harzer had despatched a strong mobile patrol from his divisional reconnaissance company south towards Nijmegen. Returning in the early hours this unit was warned by the gunners at the southern end of the Arnhem road bridge that British paratroops were on the far side. The patrol commander, *SS Hauptsturmführer* Gräbner, decided that his armoured cars and half-tracks, driven at speed, could succeed in forcing their way past the lightly armed airborne men. The leading vehicles got away with it. But as soon as Frost's men realized what was happening they gave the following vehicles a warm welcome. There ensued, the CO said afterwards, 'the most lovely battle you have ever seen. Sixteen half-track vehicles and armoured cars advanced. There they were, these awful Boches, with their pot helmets sticking out. When we dealt with them they smoked and burned in front of us almost to the end of the battle.' They were engaged at point-blank range by 6-pounder anti-tank guns, PIATs* and anti-tank grenades. An eyewitness wrote: 'The first armoured half-track went by with a rush, but we managed to land a grenade in it. The second came on with its machine-guns blazing, and a man beside me was killed before we could stop it by killing the driver and co-driver. The crew of six tried to get out and were shot one by one, lying round the half-track as it stood there in the middle of the road. Ten minutes later two came on together, firing everything they had, in an attempt to force the passage. As the leader passed the one that was already knocked out, we shot the driver. He must have been only wounded, as he promptly put it in reverse and collided with the one behind. They got inextricably entangled and we poured a hail of fire into the milling mass, whereupon one went on fire.'

The fighting was not generally so favourable for the men at the bridge. Fire from 20 mm and 40 mm flak guns, mortars, heavy artillery and small arms dominated their positions, making movement difficult and causing steadily mounting casualties. Counter-attacks came frequently. Infantry, supported by tanks or half-tracks, infiltrated through the gardens and smashed houses till beaten off by fire or driven out at the point of the bayonet. One small action was typical – 'The Germans brought up a machine-gun and poked it through a window, spraying everyone in the room. Fortunately I was beside the window, where I shot the gunner and reversed the gun on the mob outside. Grenades were now coming in at all the windows and the din was terrific. I took my sergeant and six men into the garden where we mixed it in the bushes. The enemy had no stomach for cold steel and retired to the house next door, where we followed him up with grenades.' But tough though their situation was, 2nd Parachute Battalion and attached troops had the satisfaction of being on their objective; they understood exactly what they were required to do; and they still nourished hope that they would be reinforced by the

---

* Projector, Infantry, Anti-Tank: a primitive shoulder-controlled infantry weapon capable of destroying a tank, given short range, great skill and remarkable luck.

main body of 1st Division and, later, relieved by XXX Corps. Elsewhere, the situation of 1st Airborne Division was, to say the least, confused and frustrating.

Lieutenant-Colonel Charles Mackenzie, the chief staff officer at divisional headquarters, decided on the morning of the 18th that General Urquhart must be regarded as missing and accordingly he summoned Brigadier Hicks, Commander of 1st Airlanding Brigade, to take command of the Division. Hicks was not to be envied. Information was scarce, but two facts were clear enough: the divisional plan was failing, and everywhere the initiative was slipping into the hands of a capable enemy. Regaining this initiative was obviously the paramount need, so that by one means or another the Division might still accomplish its mission. This was easier said than done, for, of the troops available, 1st and 3rd Parachute Battalions were embroiled in the outskirts of Arnhem, apparently unable to progress, and 1st Airlanding Brigade was fully stretched securing the landing zones against increasingly strong and frequent German attacks. 4th Parachute Brigade was due to land at 1000 hours but, as though to make a difficult problem impossible, news arrived from the UK Base that bad weather had forced a postponement: the Brigade would not now jump till 1500 hours.

Hicks decided that the delay in 4th Brigade's arrival made some immediate action by troops on the ground necessary, even though this meant risking the security of the landing zones. He ordered the 2nd South Staffordshires – the glider battalion with two of its companies still awaited in the second lift – to reinforce 1st and 3rd Parachute Battalions in their efforts to break through to the bridge. In the circumstances, this was probably the best that could be done prior to the arrival of the second lift. Unhappily the same cannot be said of Brigadier Hicks's plans for divisional deployment after 4th Parachute Brigade's arrival. Lift Two introduced to the battle a fresh parachute brigade, and once the paratroops and gliders were down 1st Airlanding Brigade could be released from its role of guarding the western zones. Thus the forces available to smash a passage through to the bridge suddenly rose from one to three brigades. Given that 1st Parachute Brigade was nearly expended, nevertheless the opportunity to re-shape the plan of battle and regain the initiative was real. It was not taken. Instead,

Hicks allowed 4th Parachute Brigade to persist in the now some-what irrelevant task of seizing the high ground north of Arnhem, but he ordered a re-organization that weakened their slim chances of success. He ordered that 11th Parachute Battalion be detached from 4th Brigade on landing, and proceed along with the two remaining companies of the South Staffords to beef up the piece-meal reinforcement of 1st Parachute Brigade. He gave no new tasks to 1st Airlanding Brigade. It was as though Hicks realized that the vital task was to get re-inforcements to Frost at the bridge but felt that, in his acting capacity of divisional commander, he lacked authority to divert 4th Parachute and 1st Airlanding Bri-gades to this single purpose.

In the same way that the German Army was quick to respond to the Allied landings, so the *Luftwaffe* promptly re-deployed its fighters and flak artillery to cover the aircraft routes used by the troop-carriers. So when 4th Parachute Brigade in their Dakotas and the long stream of converted bombers towing gliders ap-proached their destination they received a far hotter reception than Lift One the previous day. The second-in-command of the 11th Parachute Battalion's experience was not unique. 'Suddenly, it seemed right from beneath our feet, a crackling noise was instantly followed by a whip-like explosion. The plane lurched violently, flung us sprawling, then righted again. No need to ask if we'd been hit – we knew it. The air-burst tore a great rent in the fuselage and wounded two of my lads in the legs. The American crew chief standing by the door was only partly saved by some armour-plating. We barely had time to unhook our casualties and move them to the back of the plane when we got the green light to drop. I was glad to go. I suppose we could not have been in the air more than thirteen seconds, but that was enough. The Jerry tracer came streaking among us: I never felt more like a sitting pigeon than I did then.'

Brigadier Hackett landed safely and took half a dozen prisoners before he reached his rendezvous. It was there that he was met by Mackenzie, who had been sent by Hicks to convey the change of plan affecting the 11th Battalion. Hackett was senior to Hicks and was unaware that Urquhart had stipulated that Hicks was to take over in the event that he was incapacitated. Hackett was also a forceful leader, academically gifted, but lacking talent for suffering foolishness gladly. Certain aspects of the divisional plans he regarded as foolish, and he regretted very much that one of his parachute battalions was to be removed from his command. Mackenzie's mission was therefore not easy. Nevertheless Hackett complied with the instruction and issued orders accordingly.

The 11th Parachute Battalion set off together with the two South Stafford companies and, after being kept waiting near divisional headquarters for nearly three hours, in due course succeeded in making contact with what was left of the 1st Battalion. In the early hours of 19 September near the Elizabeth Hospital, the COs of the two parachute battalions and the South Staffords held conference. As no overall commander had been appointed for this group, they had no alternative to making plans by discussion. Their decision was to resume the advance on two routes at 0400 hours: the South Staffords would advance into Arnhem on the centre road; the 11th, led by the remnants of the 1st, would move down to the river bank, turn left, and make their way towards the bridge on Frost's old route. The Polish Parachute Brigade was due to land on DZ 'K', just south of the bridge, later on the 19th, so even at this late stage the defenders of the northern end might receive much-needed help.

The other battalions of 4th Parachute Brigade, under Hackett's command, set about their task of seizing the high ground north of Arnhem. By the early hours of 19 September the 156th Parachute Battalion had reached Wolfheze station. Hackett visited Hicks at divisional headquarters that night and it was decided that his Brigade should, on the 19th, secure the high ground at Koepel, a mile north-west of the outskirts of Arnhem, and keep control of the road leading westwards to Ede.

Meanwhile, in the area of 3rd Parachute Battalion's frustrated attempts to break through to the bridge, General Urquhart was extricating himself from the situation which had kept him so long from his headquarters. The situation arose during the 18th out of a spirited dash across a road by the General and Brigadier Lathbury which ended with the latter lying wounded in enemy-infested territory. Urquhart and a Captain Taylor carried the temporarily incapacitated Brigadier to the nearest house and laid him in the cellar. Suddenly the General looked through the window and found himself eyeball to eyeball with a German soldier. It was a case of the quick and the dead: Urquhart drew his revolver and shot the intruder. At Lathbury's repeated request Urquhart and Taylor moved next door, where their chances of escape might be better. Now followed a long and frustrating wait: the two officers could not leave the new house because an enemy self-propelled gun was parked in front of the door. But in the darkness which preceded dawn on the 19th the two officers slipped away. Their luck was good: within a few minutes a jeep appeared and on it they were quickly driven back to divisional headquarters. So, in the early morning of the third day of the battle, Urquhart resumed command and Hicks returned to 1st Airlanding Brigade.

The 19th of September dawned with 4th Parachute Brigade poised to strike eastwards to the high ground at Koepel; the South Staffords and the 1st and 11th Parachute Battalions determined to break through to the bridge; the Polish Parachute Brigade due to land south of the bridge; and Frost's 2nd Battalion still holding the northern bridge extension. With General Urquhart back in command, 1st Airborne Division seemed for a brief moment to be regaining the initiative. Two factors combined to shatter this hope. Bad weather in England grounded the American Dakotas, so the Polish Brigade's paratroops' arrival was postponed 24 hours. And on the ground the airborne infantry who were preparing to attack were almost completely without support, while the German defenders had built up their strength in tanks, half-tracks, guns and infantry.

As soon as he had been briefed up to date by his staff, Urquhart realized that, with Lathbury *hors de combat*, the advance by the Staffords and parachute battalions lacked any form of co-ordination. So he ordered Colonel Hilary Barlow, Hicks's deputy, to take command of this sector. Barlow set out by jeep to this assignment but never arrived, nor was he ever again seen. The advance went ahead as planned by the three battalion commanders. On the main road into Arnhem the South Staffords were held up at a museum, referred to by the soldiers as 'the Monastery'. They suffered severely as German tanks fired down the street while German infantry outflanked them by moving through back gardens.

43

Once they had expended their PIAT ammunition the Staffords were powerless against the panzers, and their leading company was overrun. The Battalion then attacked Den Brink which, if held by our forces, would allow the parachute battalions a far easier run on their southern route. Again, the German tanks and infantry counter-attacked, this time defeating both the South Staffords and the 11th Battalion, who were taken in the flank. Lacking co-ordination, and fighting without even the light support weapons organic to the Brigade organization, the *ad hoc* force shared the fate of the 1st and 3rd Parachute Battalions: they failed to penetrate the German defence and soon found themselves, reduced in strength to a fraction of their original total, fighting desperately for survival.

Meanwhile Hackett's Brigade was attempting its task. 156th Parachute Battalion was advancing towards Koepel and 10th Parachute Battalion was making for the Arnhem–Ede road about two miles to the north-west. The 156th attacked twice, neither time with success. Casualties were high, A Company losing all its officers. The 10th got themselves astride the road and dug in, there to endure fierce local counter-attacks. During these engagements the conduct of Captain Lionel Queripel was outstanding. At one stage a British anti-tank gun which had fallen into enemy hands was menacing the paratroop positions. The gun was supported by two machine guns but nevertheless Queripel led an attack in which he personally killed the three Germans operating the captured weapon, which was taken back into British use.

During the afternoon General Urquhart visited 4th Parachute Brigade. Seeing that they were unable to make progress on their present axis, and knowing already that the advance towards the bridge was failing, he had to come to terms with a sombre reality: his Division simply did not possess the capability to achieve its original mission. The 2nd Battalion would have to hold out at the bridge as long as it could, if possible until XXX Corps arrived, and it would have to fight its battle unaided. Urquhart decided that the remnants of his Division had better be pulled together around his headquarters in Oosterbeek to form a perimeter with its base resting on the Rhine, and stretching north some two miles. He therefore ordered Hackett to disengage 4th Brigade and move south. Orders were subsequently issued to the Airlanding Brigade and to the battalions battling on the outskirts of Arnhem to withdraw to form the new perimeter.

To withdraw whilst in close contact with an aggressive enemy is one of the most difficult manoeuvres of war. 4th Parachute Brigade achieved it but at terrible cost. As the 10th Battalion withdrew Queripel, who by this stage in the battle had already received wounds in the face and both arms, found himself cut off with a small party of men. He realized that, if he could hold the Germans for a short while, the remainder of the Battalion would have a better chance of breaking clear. A brave rearguard action was fought and then another, in which Queripel remained alone, covering the escape of the men who had fought beside him. He was killed in this final action. Across the Brigade's front many similar small battles were enacted. Whilst this disengagement was being accomplished, gliders suddenly appeared overhead. These belonged to the Polish Brigade, whose paratroops were still waiting impatiently for the weather at their USAAF air-fields to clear. By chance the low cloud had not affected the RAF bases, so aircraft towing gliders had taken off as planned. The Polish gliders were not routed to DZ 'K' because this was deemed unsuitable for glider landings, and instead were destined for Zone 'L' that was now in the midst of heavy fighting. This time the *Luftwaffe* managed to catch the stream of tugs and gliders and a *Schwarm* of fighters pounced, as described by a Dutch observer: 'Several gliders caught fire and dived in a mad flight to the ground. One of the gliders broke up in the air like a child's toy and a jeep, an anti-tank gun and people fell out of it. When the *Messerschmitts* stopped, the forest opened up. Skirmishing Germans moved forward . . . bullets tore through the gliders' wooden walls.' By 1900 hours on 19 September rather fewer than 100 men of 10th Battalion, less than 140 of 156th Battalion and about 50 of 4th Parachute Squadron Royal Engineers reached Oosterbeek – all that remained of a 2000 strong Brigade which, for the sake of caution, had been landed eight miles from its objective. Other units joined them, forming the bridgehead north of the Rhine towards which General Horrocks's XXX Corps was later redirected during its advance northwards from Nijmegen.

IX

The Bridge

IN A COMPRESSED account of a complicated battle it is impossible to do justice to the numerous individual acts of heroism that the battle of Arnhem inspired. It was almost as though the proud and capable officers and soldiers that composed 1st Airborne Division were compensating by their personal bravery and sacrifice for the virtual collapse of the division as a coherent fighting formation within hours of the start of the action. And the aircrews also, particularly in their efforts to supply the beleaguered troops with ammunition, food and medical supplies, braved skies as fiercely defended as any in World War II, at tragic cost in men and machines. The Victoria Cross is the highest award for valour in the British Armed Forces. Five were awarded for conduct at Arnhem.* Who can estimate how many comparable acts of gallantry went unseen and unreported: fifty? five hundred? For many, the sole reward for unselfish devotion to duty was to die with spirit unvanquished.

The men who held the bridge would be the last to lay claim to any monopoly or special quality of valour. Nevertheless, by their unique achievement they distinguished themselves, their units, and the memory of the battle in a manner and to a degree that turned defeat into inspiration. Let us return to the small band still holding the bridge on the fourth day of battle, 20 September, 1944.

During the morning Colonel Frost, at his headquarters north of the bridge, was discussing plans with Major Crawley for his B Company to patrol northwards. Suddenly a shell exploded close

* The recipients are listed at Appendix 3.

beside them. Frost remembered finding himself 'lying face downwards on the ground with fiendish pain in both legs. Don Crawley was lying on his back not far away and he started to drag himself into the house, I did the same and Wicks, my batman, came to drag me in under cover. I could not resist the groans which seemed to force themselves out of me and I felt ashamed, more particularly as Don never made a sound.' The stricken officers were taken downstairs into the cellar to join the 200 and more wounded under the untiring care of Doctors James Logan and David Wright and of the Roman Catholic padre, Father Egan, whose oecumenicity in those grim circumstances was welcomed by the suffering and the dying of many faiths. Command of the bridgehead passed to Major Freddie Gough, with Major Tatham-Warter controlling the 2nd Battalion.

Even by the second and third days of fighting the number of inhabitable buildings in the area had been inexorably diminished. German tanks and guns had pounded constantly at the houses, forcing the defenders to evacuate them. By the time Frost was wounded the situation was perilous. Tanks were repeatedly firing phosphorus shells into the British positions, setting them alight: the defence was cramped into what buildings or cover remained, a fraction of the original. General Bittrich had received re-inforcements to crack the British airborne footholds north of the Rhine. These included panzer grenadier battalions experienced in house-to-house fighting, artillery of all kinds, a *Pioneer-Lehr-Bataillon* skilled in the use of flame-throwers and, most important, *Königstiger-Abteilung 503*, a panzer unit equipped with the most formidable heavy tanks in the world. To stand off this array of men and metal the 2nd Parachute Battalion Group possessed rifles, sub and light machine-guns, some PIATs, effective only at point-blank range, a few medium mortars, and the four 6-pounder anti-tank guns. Ammunition was nearly exhausted. They also enjoyed the support of the divisional light artillery, firing from the Oosterbeek area. Lieutenant-Colonel 'Sheriff' Thompson's gunners distinguished themselves throughout the battle, maintaining communications where all others failed, and firing with accurate effect. Attack after attack by German infantry, mainly across the bridge from the south or along the northern riverbank from the east, was broken up by this fire. The British had two more advantages in an otherwise hopelessly uneven contest: they were in defence and able to benefit from the built-up nature of the battlefield in the same way as Krafft's and Harzer's men had done in frustrating Lathbury's and Hackett's efforts; and their spirit and confidence were remarkable. Lieutenant Mackay, whose sappers defended the schoolhouse immediately east of the bridge extension with such skill, caught the spirit in his account: 'We drove off three attacks in two hours. The school was now like a sieve. Wherever you looked you could see daylight. Splattered everywhere was blood; it lay in pools in the rooms, it covered the smocks of the defenders and ran in small rivulets down the stairs. The men themselves were the grimmest sight of all: eyes red-rimmed for want of sleep, their faces, blackened by fire-fighting, wore three days' growth of beard. Many of them had minor wounds and their clothes were cut away to expose a roughly fixed, blood-soaked field-dressing. Looking at these men I realized I should never have to give the order "These positions will be held to the last round and the last man". They were conscious of their superiority. Around them lay four times their number of enemy dead.'*

Pressure from the east mounted throughout the day. An important sector of the defence was that held by the brigade headquarters defence platoon and signals troop, led by the staff captain, Bernard Briggs. Holding houses east of the bridge extension, they bore the brunt of many assaults. Now, one by one, these buildings were set ablaze and finally the valiant group was forced to fall back onto A Company, by now confined around the arches of the bridge itself. German tanks began to roam the streets that for three days had been unsafe for them. Identifying what was left of the British position they opened fire at point-blank range. The means of defeating them – the 6-pounders and the PIATs – were disabled or out of ammunition. As though to announce that the end was near at hand, the night of the 20th saw the death of a young officer whose courage had set an example even among Frost's dedicated soldiers: he was Lieutenant J. H. Grayburn.

On the first evening of the battle, soon after the 2nd Parachute

* Mackay's account first appeared in *Blackwood's Magazine* in October 1945. For an Arnhem bibliography, see Appendix 4.

Battalion had captured the northern end of the bridge, A Company launched two attacks across the bridge to secure the southern part. The first, led by Lieutenant McDermot, was halted by fire from a hitherto silent pillbox and an armoured car. Grayburn tried later but his platoon suffered eight casualties in the first 50 yards. Although wounded in the shoulder, Grayburn continued to press the attack with the greatest dash and fortitude until casualties became so heavy that he was forced to withdraw. Disregarding his wound, he continued to command his platoon. Three days later, on the 20th, his platoon position was brought under such heavy fire that he withdrew north. But, seeing that the Germans were attempting to lay demolition charges under the bridge, Grayburn sallied forth with a fighting patrol which drove off the enemy and gave time for the fuses to be removed. He was again wounded, this time in the back, but he refused to be taken to the dressing station. Finally an enemy tank approached so close to his position that it became untenable. He then stood up to direct the withdrawal of his platoon even though this exposed him to the tank's crew. His men succeeded in reaching the main battalion defences; Grayburn was killed that night.

Just after dark the building housing brigade headquarters was set alight. The wounded were moved to a house at the back but before the task was complete this too was ablaze. There was nowhere else for the wounded to go: reluctantly, Colonel Frost and Major Gough agreed that opposition from Brigade HQ should cease so that the wounded could be surrendered. This unavoidable decision marked the beginning of the end of organized resistance at the bridge. Not unnaturally, the Germans sought to extend the truce to which they had agreed into a general round-up of surviving paratroopers. This was resisted, but the British troops in the vicinity were in an extremely difficult position. They could not possibly shoot into the area from which their own wounded were being rescued; yet there were German soldiers moving freely to improve their tactical advantage. Tatham-Warter and Gough considered the situation and decided that 2nd Parachute Battalion should move to a nearby warehouse. The battalion strength was now nine officers and 110 soldiers, together with approximately 30 assorted engineers, gunners and other attached elements.

Reaching the warehouse, Tatham-Warter found himself under continuous German pressure and he considered it best to stay there overnight and then split his force to move in two parties at first light to re-occupy the old brigade headquarters area. But *SS Sturmbannführer* Brinkmann had also selected first light on the 21st as the moment to launch his battle-group into a final mopping-up operation in the area held by the British. While five tanks and a self-propelled gun fired into the upper storeys of the few houses still held by paratroopers,p anzer grenadiers fought skilfully through the ground floors. The crash of stick grenades preceded each attack, and often the grenadiers moved from house to house by blowing 'mouseholes' in the connecting walls, thus avoiding exposure in the streets. Even at this stage, when the troops on both sides must have known that the battle for the bridge was to all intents and purposes over, the paratroopers fought grimly. A German noted '. . . one young Britisher began to dodge about to draw our fire, while another tried to come at us from the side with a knife. One man remaining leaped at us swinging his rifle as a club'. Brinkmann's men prevailed and by degrees the British positions were overrun. Of the paratroopers who were rounded up, most were wounded. Many were nevertheless later to escape from captivity and, helped by fearless Dutch patriots, were to find their way back to safety. Theirs is another story. Tatham-Warter concluded his report of the battle with these laconic but moving words:

'It was an appalling end, I'm afraid; they had all fought so very well – particularly A Company and Bernard Briggs and his party who had borne the brunt of the fighting.'

X

Comment

THE 'APPALLING END' at Arnhem Bridge concluded one of the finest feats of arms in the annals of British military history. It did not mark the end of the battle as a whole. Five miles to the west the 1st Airborne Division fought on to hold a bridgehead north of the Rhine. The Polish Parachute Brigade, whose arrival had twice been postponed by 24 hours due to impossible weather, finally descended on 21 September under conditions which were very nearly impossible, so much so that only half the Dakotas found the DZ and delivered their loads. The DZ was not 'K' south of the bridge but a newly selected zone near the village of Driel, just south of the Rhine from the divisional perimeter, to which they were diverted by General Urquhart. As re-inforcements they were, through no fault of theirs, too few and too late. During the night of 25/26 September what was left of 1st Airborne Division withdrew south across the Rhine.

The combined attack of I Airborne Corps and XXX Corps had failed in its sweeping strategic intention of turning the German defence of the Ruhr and hastening victory in Europe. In a tactical sense it could be claimed as 90 per cent successful, having secured crossings across all but the last of the bridges chosen for capture. Before the battle the enemy had been given time to don at least a few pieces of body armour, and against these the tip of the airborne rapier snapped. Whether or not this fracture was inevitable in the circumstances will remain for ever an open question. Allied airborne tactics and techniques had been fashioned by experience of jabbing at the chinks and had never really been designed for running the opponent through. Thus the need for one commander to bear responsibility for all aspects of the enterprise – air and ground – was overlooked; the importance of close air support was insufficiently appreciated; and the value of uncommitted airborne reserves was never understood. The worth of really first-class fighting soldiers was fully recognized but this, without the other elements, was not enough.

On the first day of the battle Private McKinnon of the 3rd Parachute Battalion had entered a butcher's shop in Arnhem. The owner, having no meat, gave him bread, cheese and wine. Then he fetched his twelve-year-old daughter so that she could see the first of the English soldiers who had come from the skies to liberate Holland. She had one carefully prepared line of English to say: 'Many happy returns after your long stay away.' It was not, after all, to be a happy return. After the battle the Germans executed all Dutch civilians suspected of having assisted the British. For the survivors, and for all the Dutch north of the Rhine, the coming winter was to be a terrible season of retribution and starvation. General Urquhart ended his official account of the action with the words: 'There is no doubt that all would willingly undertake another operation under similar conditions in the future. We have no regrets.' More remarkable is the echo of his sentiment by the citizens of Arnhem and Oosterbeek, none of whom seems ever to have regretted that the attempt was made, in spite of the appalling consequences. A spirit of friendship and mutual respect between paratroopers and Dutch citizens has ever after flourished, an appropriate memorial to those who lie buried in the soil of Holland.

1st Airborne Division's Order of Battle
17 September 1944

Divisional Headquarters

General Officer Commanding	Major-General R. E. Urquhart
General Staff Officer 1 (Operations)	Lieutenant-Colonel C. B. Mackenzie
General Staff Officer 1 (Air)	Lieutenant-Colonel E. H. Steele-Baume
Assistant Adjutant and Quartermaster General	Lieutenant-Colonel P. H. H. H. Preston
Assistant Director of Medical Services	Colonel G. M. Warrack
Assistant Director of Ordnance Services	Lieutenant-Colonel G. A. Mobbs

1st Parachute Brigade   (Strength: about 2400)

Commander	Brigadier G. W. Lathbury
1st Parachute Battalion	Lieutenant-Colonel D. T. Dobie
2nd Parachute Battalion	Lieutenant-Colonel J. D. Frost
3rd Parachute Battalion	Lieutenant-Colonel J. A. C. Fitch

4th Parachute Brigade   (Strength: about 2000)

Commander	Brigadier J. W. Hackett
156th Parachute Battalion	Lieutenant-Colonel Sir W. R. de B. des Voeux
10th Parachute Battalion	Lieutenant-Colonel K. B. I. Smyth
11th Parachute Battalion	Lieutenant-Colonel G. H. Lea

21st Independent Parachute Company   Major B. A. Wilson

1st Airlanding Brigade   (Strength: about 2900)

Commander	Brigadier P. H. W. Hicks
Deputy Commander	Colonel H. N. Barlow
1st Battalion, Border Regiment	Lieutenant-Colonel T. Haddon

7th Battalion, King's Own Scottish Borderers	Lieutenant-Colonel R. Payton-Reid
2nd Battalion, South Staffordshire Regiment	Lieutenant-Colonel W. D. H. McCardie

Divisional Troops
(Strength: about 2795, including Div HQ and Independent Company)

Reconnaissance Squadron	Major C. F. H. Gough

Royal Artillery

Commander RA	Lieutenant-Colonel R. G. Loder-Symonds
1st Airlanding Light Regiment RA	Lieutenant-Colonel W. F. K. Thompson
1st Airlanding Anti-tank Battery RA	Major W. F. Arnold
2nd Airlanding Anti-tank Battery RA	Major A. F. Haynes
1st Forward Observer Unit RA	Major D. R. Wight Boycott

Royal Engineers

Commander RE	Lieutenant-Colonel E. C. W. Myers
1st Parachute squadron RE	Major D. C. Murray
4th Parachute Squadron RE	Major Ae. J. M. Perkins
9th Field Company RE	Major J. C. Winchester
261st Field Park Company RE	Major J. N. Chivers

Commander Royal Signals	Lieutenant-Colonel T. C. V. Stephenson

Royal Army Service Corps

Commander RASC	Lieutenant-Colonel M. St. J. Packe
93rd Composite Company	Major F. Tompkins
250th Light Composite Company	Major J. L. Gifford
253rd Composite Company	Major R. K. Gordon

Royal Army Medical Corps

16th Parachute Field Ambulance	Lieutenant-Colonel E. Townsend
133rd Parachute Field Ambulance	Lieutenant-Colonel W. C. Alford
181st Airlanding Field Ambulance	Lieutenant-Colonel A. T. Marrable

Royal Army Ordnance Corps
Ordnance Field Park   Major C. C. Chidgey

Royal Electrical and Mechanical Engineers
Commander REME   Lieutenant-Colonel E. J. Kinvig
Divisional Workshops   Major W. S. Carrick

Corps of Military Police
Provost Company   Major O. P. Haig

Army Air Corps
No 1 Wing, Glider Pilot Regiment   Lieutenant-Colonel I. A. Murray
No 2 Wing, Glider Pilot Regiment   Lieutenant-Colonel J. W. Place
          (Divisional strength delivered to Battle: 10095)

1st Airborne Division's Allotment of Aircraft and Gliders to Units, by Lifts

(This is the plan: adjustments were made in execution)

First Lift: 17 September 1944
Dropping Zone 'X' (see map on page 62)
'H' – 20 minutes* – six Stirling aircraft of 38 Group RAF to drop pathfinders of 21st Independent Parachute Company.
'H' Hour – 149 C-47 aircraft of IX US Troop Carrier Command to drop 1st Parachute Brigade.

Landing Zone 'S'
'H' – 20 minutes – six Stirling aircraft of 38 Group RAF to drop pathfinders of 21st Independent Parachute Company.
'H' Hour – 153 aircraft of 46 and 38 Groups RAF to release 153 Horsa gliders carrying most of 1st Airlanding Brigade Group.

Landing Zone 'Z'
'H' Hour – 167 aircraft of 38 Group RAF to release 154 Horsa and 13 Hamilcar gliders carrying Divisional Tactical Headquarters and Divisional Troops.

Total First Lift
161 parachute aircraft
320 towing aircraft
320 gliders (13 Hamilcar, 307 Horsa)

Second Lift: 18 September 1944
Dropping Zone 'Y'
126 C-47 aircraft of IX US Troop Carrier Command to drop most of 4th Parachute Brigade.

Landing Zone 'X'
208 aircraft of 38 and 46 Groups RAF to release 189 Horsa, 4 Waco CG-4A, and 15 Hamilcar gliders carrying Divisional Troops.

* 'H' Hour is the time at which the main body of the Division starts to land: 'H' – 20 minutes is 20 minutes prior to 'H' Hour.

Landing Zone 'S'
62 aircraft of 46 Group RAF to release 62 Horsa gliders carrying elements of 1st Airlanding Brigade Group.

Dropping Zone 'L'
35 aircraft of 38 Group RAF to drop supplies.

Total Second Lift
126 parachute aircraft
270 towing aircraft
270 gliders (15 Hamilcar, 4 CG-4A, 251 Horsa)
 35 supply-dropping aircraft

Third Lift: 19 September 1944

Dropping Zone 'K'
114 C-47 aircraft of IX US Troop Carrier Command to drop most of 1st Polish Parachute Brigade.

Landing Zone 'L'
45 aircraft of 38 Group RAF to release 35 Horsa and 10 Hamilcar gliders carrying elements of 1st Polish Parachute Brigade Group and 878th US Airborne Aviation Engineer Battalion.

Dropping Zone 'V'
163 aircraft and 38 and 46 Groups RAF to drop supplies.

Total Third Lift
114 parachute aircraft
 45 towing aircraft
 45 gliders (10 Hamilcar, 35 Horsa)
163 supply-dropping aircraft

Totals - Three Lifts Combined
Aircraft Sorties

dropping paratroops	401
releasing gliders	635
dropping supplies	198
Total	1234

Gliders Released

Hamilcars	38
Horsas	593
CG-4As	4
Total	635

Victoria Crosses Awarded for Gallantry at Arnhem

Of the five Victoria Crosses awarded for gallantry in the operation, four were posthumous – Captain L. E. Queripel, The Royal Sussex Regiment, attached to 10th Parachute Battalion; Flight-Lieutenant D. A. S. Lord, 271 Squadron 46 Group RAF; Lieutenant J. H. Grayburn, 2nd Parachute Battalion; and Lance Sergeant J. D. Baskeyfield, 2nd Battalion The South Staffordshire Regiment. The fifth was awarded to Major R. H. Cain, The Royal Northumberland Fusiliers, attached to 2nd Battalion the South Staffordshire Regiment, who received his decoration from His Majesty King George VI.

Bibliography

Arnhem Municipality. *The Battle of Arnhem*. 1946.

Bauer, Cornelis. *The Battle of Arnhem – The Betrayal Myth Refuted*. Hodder and Stoughton 1969.

Chatterton, George S. *The Wings of Pegasus*. MacDonald & Co. Ltd. 1962.

Farrar-Hockley, Anthony. *Airborne Carpet*. (Purnell's WWII Battle Book No 9) 1969.

Gibson, Staff Sergeant R. *Nine days* (17–25 September 1944). Arthur H. Stockwell, Ltd. 1956.

Hagen, L. *Arnhem Lift* (A Glider Pilot's Account). 2nd Edition. Pilot Press 1953.

Hibbert, Christopher. *The Battle of Arnhem*. Batsford 1962.

HM Stationary Office. *By Air to Battle*. London 1945.

Mackay, E. M. 'The Battle of Arnhem Bridge', *Blackwood's Magazine*. October 1945.

McKee, A. *The Race for the Rhine Bridges: 1940; 1944; 1945*. Published 1971.

Mackenzie, Charles. *It was like this: a short factual account of the Battle of Arnhem*. 4th Edition. Adremo CV 1960.

Norton, Geoffrey. *The Red Devils* (The Story of British Airborne Forces). Famous Regiments Series. Leo Cooper 1971.

Ryan, Cornelius. *A Bridge Too Far*. Hamish Hamilton 1974.

Saunders, Hilary St George. *The Red Beret* (Story of the Parachute Regiment at War 1940–1945). Michael Joseph 1950.

Tugwell, Maurice. *Airborne to Battle* (A History of Airborne Warfare 1918–1971). William Kimber 1971.

Urquhart, Roy. *Arnhem*. Cassell 1958.

War Office. *Airborne Forces* (The Second World War – Army – Series). Compiled by Lieutenant-Colonel T. B. H. Otway, DSO. 1951.

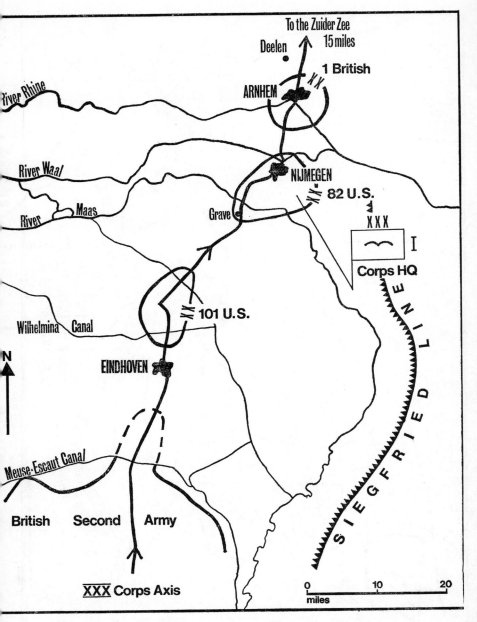

Operation Market Garden – the 'Airborne Carpet' as planned.

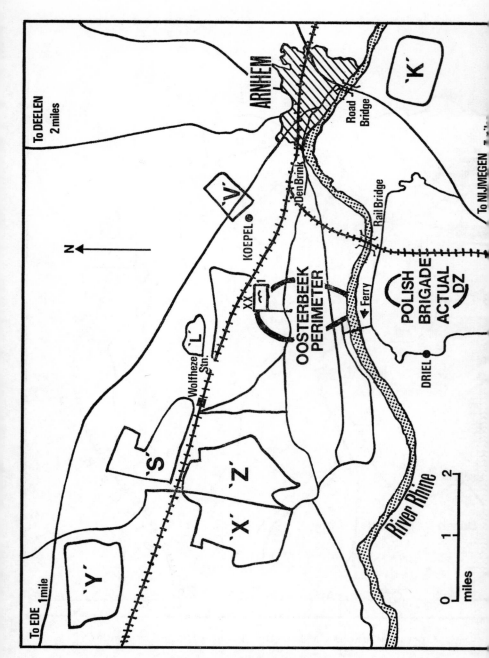

Arnhem and the Landing Zones.

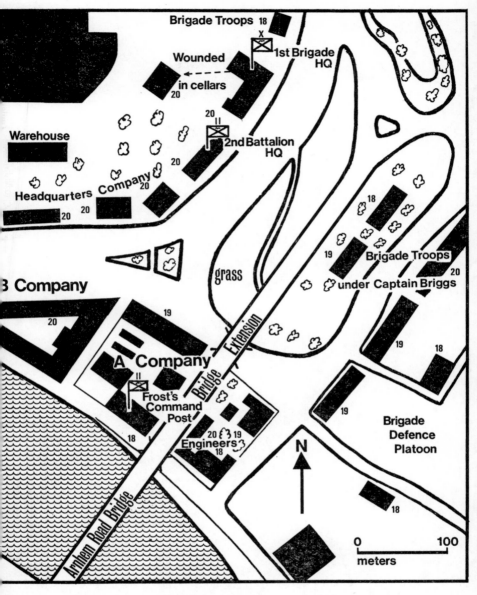

The Defence of Arnhem Bridge – 17–21 September 1944.

Figures denote date building destroyed by enemy action or otherwise made untenable by British. Troops fell back onto A Company and finally onto Headquarters Company positions.